Old KILMACOLM & BRIDGE OF WEIR

by
Wilson Holland

Kilmacolm from the north, *c*.1910. The parish's name is held to mean 'the cell of my dear Columba' and the first settlement here was probably in the seventh or eighth century and ecclesiastical in nature. It remained a mere hamlet until the mid-nineteenth century when the railway arrived, completely transforming it. An indication of the rapid effect the railway had can be seen in the village's population figures – in 1871 there were only 395 inhabitants but ten years later the number had leapt to 1,170.

© Wilson Holland 1998
First published in the United Kingdom, 1998,
by Stenlake Publishing, Ochiltree Sawmill, The Lade,
Ochiltree, Ayrshire, KA18 2NX
Telephone / Fax: 01290 423114

ISBN 1 84033 040 6

The area's first bus service was introduced in 1925 by the Port Glasgow Motor Company (later renamed as the Pioneer Bus Company). This ran between Port Glasgow, Langbank and Kilmacolm and was so successful that services expanded rapidly. However, it wasn't long before Bridge of Weir's local bus company, Garners, was operating on the routes between the village and Glasgow and Paisley.

FOREWORD

The villages of Kilmacolm and Bridge of Weir are set only three and a half miles apart and between them stand the world famous Quarrier's Orphan Homes. However, despite their proximity, the two villages have developed separately. Kilmacolm has a lengthy – if largely uneventful – history stretching back centuries, while Bridge of Weir has only really emerged since the eighteenth century. Nevertheless, since the arrival of the railways, they have shared a common purpose as dormitory towns for the business people of Glasgow and the other big towns of the region. Over the last 150 years, these wealthy inhabitants have ensured that both villages have the distinction of fine open streets and impressive residential architecture. Much of it, in the heyday of the early years of the century, is on display in this book.

I would like to thank all those who have previously written about this area. The Rev. Mr Murray's 1907 *History of Kilmacolm* and two books on the history of Quarrier's Homes, Alexander Gammie's *William Quarrier and the Story of the Orphan Homes of Scotland* (1937) and Anna Magnusson's *The Village – A History of Quarrier's* (1984), have provided invaluable information. The late William Lyle's 1975 book *Bridge of Weir* will, of course, need no introduction to anyone interested in the past and present of the village.

Wilson Holland

St. Columba U.F. Church, Kilmalcolm

In the late nineteenth century Kilmacolm's Free Church congregation built St Columba Church which would remain in use until 1957 when the congregation united with that of St James' in Duchal Road. St James' was henceforth renamed St Columba and the old church was left disused until it was demolished.

Cross, Kilmacolm

509/81

Kilmacolm Cross, long before the intrusion of the motor car. The stone memorial well on the far side commemorates the founding of the village's waterworks system which went into operation in 1878 and which was enlarged in 1900. The village already had a gas supply which was installed in 1873 and this powered the village's streetlamps, the first of which were erected in 1876. The electricity supply was introduced in 1904.

4

The Cross, Kilmacolm

Postal services were also rapidly improved as Kilmacolm's new status as a dormitory town emerged. The town's first post office was opened in 1851 and had been a relatively quiet concern, run by an elderly postmistress from a thatched cottage. However, with the town's expansion, demands were soon made for a more up-to-date operation: the old woman was removed in favour of a more youthful and capable replacement while the thatched cottage was demolished and the office later rehoused at the Cross.

Market Place with Parish Church, Kilmacolm

The Parish Church was erected in 1833 on the site of its predecessor which had been declared to be in a 'most dangerous state'. The new church was designed to seat 1,000 and was initially far too large for the congregation. But as the years passed and the population expanded, it then became too small. In 1875 the clock and a bell were installed in the tower and fifteen years later a vestry was added, the stonework of which includes a small portion of masonry from a twelfth century chapel that had once been on the site. There were further extensions at the southern end of the building between 1902 and 1903.

The children's playground at the rear of the Parish Church, seen here in 1926 with the massive tower of the Hydropathic Hotel rising above the trees. In 1922 the ground adjoining the playground became the site of the town's first local authority development of eight houses.

Opened in 1880, the 128-roomed Hydropathic Hotel represented the last word in elegance. But it had an uncertain beginning when the company in ownership collapsed after only three years and the building had to be sold at a third of its original cost of £47,000. Nevertheless, it survived and was a successful venture for many years until it was severely damaged in the 'hurricane' of 1968. This, allied to the fact that the hotel could not get a full alcohol licence, led to its closure and eventual demolition in 1974.

The approach to the Cross from Lochwinnoch Road. The Kilmacolm Institute was opened in 1921 in what was formerly the Buchanan Arms Hotel. The hotel had to close the year before because of the fashion for temperance which had taken hold of the community – a vote had been taken on the issue of banning alcohol in the village and, amazingly, well over half the population voted in favour. The Institute contained bathing facilities for men, a billiard room, library and a canteen. For the ladies there was a room provided with sewing machines, electric irons and other luxury household appliances. The council bought the property in 1958 and reopened it as the town's community centre.

The Octavia Buildings are almost totally unchanged since this picture was taken in 1901 soon after they were built.

The tenements at Norval Place were constructed in 1873 and are largely unchanged today.

Commonly known as the 'English Church', the St Fillan's Episcopal Church on the left was replaced by the present church, also called St Fillan's, in 1954.

Station Road, 1926. Before the railway arrived in 1869 Kilmacolm was a remote hamlet. A description of the mid-nineteenth century recorded that it had around forty thatched weather-beaten houses, a shop or two, several ale houses, a smithy and its kirk. It was also noted that, presumably because of its 'airy situation', quite a few of the inhabitants had managed to live beyond the age of 70. The only drawback was the moist climate which affected most houses with damp and caused a prevalence of rheumatic and inflammatory diseases amongst the villagers.

The railway from Glasgow arrived in Bridge of Weir in 1864 but it was another five years before it was extended to Greenock, reaching Kilmacolm on the way. The Kilmacolm – Greenock section was closed to passenger traffic in 1959 and in 1983 the whole section from Glasgow was closed. Around 1990 the railbed was converted into part of the cycling and walking track that runs from Glasgow to Greenock via Paisley.

The Lochwinnoch Road. The railway brought to Kilmacolm many new wealthier inhabitants. These were mostly Glasgow businessmen and, after tearing down most of the old cottages, they built for themselves new houses that befitted their status. Of particular note is 'Windyhill' which was constructed between 1899 and 1906 using designs by Charles Rennie Mackintosh. Built for William Davidson, a discerning patron of the arts, it was Mackintosh's first independent commission for a house.

Birkmyre Park was presented to the village in 1890 by Adam Birkmyre, owner of the Clyde Canvas and Ropework in Greenock. Its laying out cost £7,000. He lived in the house overlooking the park, known as 'Shallot', which now contains the Primary Section of the St Columba private school.

THE MILL, KILMACOLM

Pacemure Mill is still standing although this view of it from the River Gryffe is now obscured by more recent buildings. The river takes its name from an ancient word for grief, reputedly in reference to the casualties of some great unrecorded battle that took place along its banks.

BATHING POOL, BALROSSIE, KILMACOLM.

A. 4840.

This swimming pool belongs to the Balrossie School. Later a list D school, it was founded as an orphan home for sailors' children on the lands of Balrossie farm, also known as Slates, in 1898. Education had always been well catered for in Kilmacolm Parish. Even as far back as the 1830s there were six schools, including the parochial one in the village. These all taught the elementary subjects of reading, writing and arithmetic. It was noted at the time that 'more was seldom required' and there was nobody in the parish who could not read.

In the early years of the century there were two nurseries in the town. This commercial glasshouse belonged to Stoddart's nurseries and tomatoes were the likely crop.

Golf Club House, Kilmacolm

Kilmacolm's golf course was opened in 1891 on the lands of A.A. Speirs of Elderslie and was laid out by William Campbell. The course's hilly location, beside the Glen Moss area of Kilmacolm, makes it one of the most popular and scenic courses in the west of Scotland.

Glenmosston Model Farm, Kilmacolm

Before the mid-nineteenth century agriculture was the main employer and there were enough small farms in the area to merit the formation of the Kilmacolm Farmer Society in 1793. But despite this, most of the farms were run using primitive methods and the area was slow to catch on to the improvements which were being introduced in other parts of the country. By the 1830s, the area had begun to shake off its poor reputation but this new prosperity was short-lived for some as the village's expansion would soon swallow up a number of the smaller farms. Model farms such as this were well managed concerns usually based on the outskirts of cities so that urban children could come and see how rural life worked.

This picture of Rowantree Hill Farm gives a good idea of the sort of buildings that were around before the railway arrived. However, it became one of the many that fell victim to the new development of the town as a quarry was started on its lands. As luck would have it a great dolerite dyke runs from Haddockstone in Houston Parish to Rashielee in Inchinnan Parish and the 'whin-gaws' (as colliers called such dykes) provided much of the stone used to build the new houses and roads. There were two other quarries in the town: Gowkhouse in the town centre and Auchenbothie to the north (now the site of a Cala Homes development).

Born in Greenock in 1829, William Quarrier spent a childhood of poverty in Glasgow; but later, as owner of three shoe shops, became a successful businessman. He resolved never to forget the squalor of his own youth and decided to devote himself to helping the many orphans he found roaming the streets of Glasgow. His first orphanage was opened in the city in 1871. Quarrier felt that the care offered by large orphanages was inadequate and set about developing the concept of Cottage Homes. These would house small numbers of children who could live together under the care of a housemother and housefather. As a result the first Cottage Home was opened near Bridge of Weir in 1878 and by the 1890s the complex contained more than 50 cottages along with a school, church, dairy, poultry farm and workshops.

Dinner time in the Lincoln and Garfield cottage. The Homes relied on charity and each new cottage was generally named at the donor's suggestion. There was one name, however, that William Quarrier would refuse to allow and that was his own. A devout Christian, he insisted that the buildings belonged to God, not him!

GENERAL STORE, ORPHAN HOMES OF SCOTLAND, BRIDGE OF WEIR.

Training the orphans for adult life was a key function of the homes and children received training in the drapery and general stores. The original aim was that each child should leave the Homes having learned a trade. For the boys there were apprenticeships in joinery, carpentry, shoemaking, printing etc. and for the girls there were the sewing and laundry rooms and the opportunity to help out with the domestic upkeep of the Homes. Ultimately, many of the children were given the opportunity to forge a new life in one of the Empire's colonies and between the opening of the complex and 1938 about 7,000 youngsters were sent to Canada. Today, it is estimated that more than 200,000 Canadians can trace their roots back to the little village in Renfrewshire.

DRAPERY STORE, ORPHAN HOMES OF SCOTLAND, BRIDGE OF WEIR.

Quarrier was also concerned that the Homes should have some provision for the sick, in particular those suffering from tuberculosis and epilepsy. He opened Scotland's first Consumption Sanatorium at the complex in 1898 and just before his death in 1903 made provision for an epilepsy colony which was opened in 1906.

An elementary education was something that Quarrier promised the children who were sent to his Homes. However, this like everything else in the enterprise was paid for by charity funds and Quarrier was enraged when in 1898 he received a demand from the Kilmacolm School Board for four years back payment of parish and school rates – even though they had contributed nothing to the education of the Homes' children. In reaction to this he decided to embarrass the school board and he marched 800 children to Kilmacolm School where, because of their enormous number, they were refused admission. He made his point but it would be several years before the board finally agreed to take responsibility for education at the Homes.

Positioned behind the Central Building was the *James Arthur*, a sailing ship specially built and cemented into the ground for the Homes in 1887. James Arthur was a prominent businessman (his statue stands in the grounds of Glasgow Cathedral) and his wife, by way of commemorating him, paid for the construction of the ship. Thirty boys lived and worked on it in preparation for a life in the Merchant Navy and were trained by a housefather who was once a sea-faring captain. The ship was removed about 1913 and its site was taken by a variety of different concerns, including a printworks, a scout hut and a kiosk for serving afternoon tea to visitors to the Homes.

FIRE BRIGADE PRACTICE

Construction of the Homes' Fire Station was funded by Coats of Paisley. There were two horse-drawn fire pumps and these were manned by housefathers.

The Homes' Mount Zion Church was opened in 1888. Originally, it could seat 1,000 but two subsequent extensions meant that by the 1930s the capacity was raised to over 2,600.

Bridge of Weir owes its existence to the establishment of cotton and flax mills in the late eighteenth century, but it was not until the arrival of the railway in 1864 that the place began to expand. From then on the businessmen of Glasgow and Greenock began to move in and by 1900 their homes were spread from the centre of the village to Ranfurly Hill above.

A turn of the century view of Main Street at its intersection with Torr Road.

A number of these buildings at the Burngill have now been demolished. At one time it was the location of the Brig Inn Hostelry where stagecoaches could stop and change horses.

The first mansions in Bridge of Weir were built on Ranfurly Hill, separated from the 'original' village by the railway. This division in the community was psychological as well as physical and the village's entry in the Statistical Account of the 1950s noted a palpable antipathy amongst some villagers who lived in the centre towards the wealthy inhabitants on the hill. As many of the villagers worked in the big houses the differences were no doubt based on class but there were criticisms that their rich neighbours took little interest in local affairs.

The exclusivity of Horsewood Road at Ranfurly has long since been invaded by more recent housing on the hillside in the foreground.

The cross-roads at the Horsewood. Just over the hill in the background stands the ruin of the fifteenth century Ranfurly Castle. The Knox family owned the lands from the 1440s and lived there for over 200 years. The castle was a ruin by the beginning of the nineteenth century although apparently one of its wings still had a roof on it.

The club house of Ranfurly Castle Golf Club was built in 1904-05, although the original plan to have a clock tower attached was never carried out. There was already a course at Ranfurly, although not much older, which then became known as The Old Course, Ranfurly Golf Club. At one time there was also a Ladies Club and out by Locher there was the Thistle Golf Club. This club, assisted by the directors of the Tannery for their employees who played there, rented its grounds from a farmer but during the Second World War they reverted back to farmland and the course was never reopened. Most of the members then joined the Old Course club.

Ranfurly Hotel was opened in 1882 but due to poor business it closed down before the First World War. It was then used to accommodate the homeless and during the war wounded soldiers were billeted there. In 1920 it became a private school but this closed five years later. After lying empty for some time it was then developed into shops and flats.

In its first years as a hotel the Ranfurly's guests were mostly visitors from Glasgow and beyond. By express train it was only 22 minutes from the city and guests could enjoy beautifully kept gardens with panoramic views and a bowling green. Fishing, golf, and walking were further attractions and an 1898 advertisement stated that a coffee room, drawing room, billiard room, extra bedrooms and a conservatory had all been recently added to the existing facilities.

A view of Bridge of Weir from Houstonhead Dam, *c*.1935.

Built across the road from Ranfurly Hotel in 1877-78, St Machar's Church was originally only a chapel of ease and had to wait nine years before being granted full parish status. Later, the congregation united with that of Ranfurly church and it became known as St Machar's Ranfurly. Below it was the village's railway station which was always busy with freight on its way to Port Glasgow and Greenock from Glasgow.

The Gryffe Viaduct at Bridge of Weir was built in 1868-69 and today it forms part of the Glasgow to Greenock path and cycleway.

Based in the centre of the village, Garner's main services ran to Paisley via Georgetown. There was also a service from the railway station to the Orphan Homes. The company's owner, Dolly Garner, died in the late 1960s but services continued for several more years before the business finally ceased. The site of the Central Garage has now been taken by a supermarket.

LOCHER MILL, BRIDGE OF WEIR

Lochermill (as it is spelled on Ordnance Survey maps) was at one time a farm and is not to be confused with the Locher printworks and bleachfield up-river which is now a leather tannery. The outhouses have now been converted into houses although the main farmhouse has gone.

Cotton mills were originally the main industry of the town and by the 1830s there were seven of them in the area. Of these the biggest were Findlay's which employed 94 people (this later became the premises of the Gryffe Tannery) and the Gryffe Mill which had 260 staff.

The cotton mills all closed around the mid-nineteenth century but it wasn't long before the leather trade became the mainstay of economic life in Bridge of Weir. This is the Gryffe Tannery which was in business from 1870 until it was destroyed in 1904 by a fire which destroyed two other adjacent tanning works as well. Today the tannery trade is represented by the Clydesdale Works of the Bridge of Weir Leather Co. Ltd and the National Chrome Tanning Co. Ltd.

Although Houston Road remains mostly unchanged from this 1947 view, the hillside in the background has since been taken up by housing. Many houses in the centre of the village had been condemned before 1939 but by 1950 most had not yet been replaced. By 1959 about 300 council houses had been built but there were criticisms that many of them were too far from the village centre and important amenities such as the shops and the school.

North Street, Houston

Houston's history, despite being as unremarkable as that of both Kilmacolm and Bridge of Weir, stretches back to the thirteenth century when it was a cluster of dwellings around the castle of Hugo de Kilpeter (i.e. Hew's toun). Nevertheless by 1760 the population of its entire parish was still only 300. In 1781 the castle was partly demolished and stone from it was used in the building of a New Town of 35 houses. As a result various mills and the Houston Bleachfield opened in the area and the population subsequently increased to a peak of over 2,500 in 1831. However, by the end of the nineteenth century this number had already started to drop. As the railway bypassed the town, it was never subject to the same developments enjoyed by its neighbouring villages and by 1905 the bleachfield had closed and the village had reverted back to agriculture, its original way of making a living.

By 1950 Houston's population had dropped to 600, hardly even enough to support its three pubs. However, a growing problem at the time was the invasion of drinkers from Glasgow and Paisley who travelled in on weekend evenings and then caused havoc on the late buses home. In the fifties there were also plans to build a New Town which would take the overspill from Greenock, Port Glasgow and Renfrew and had these succeeded the target population would have been 40,000. But Houston remained a sleepy rural community and even today retains an anachronistic pack of foxhounds. It perhaps enjoyed one advantage over it neighbouring villages, as Rev. Heron noted in the 1950s, and that was that it remained a 'real community', untouched by outside influences and incomers from the cities.